T0196918

POWER OF
DESTINY

POWER OF DESTINY

POETRY

KARRAN DEOKARRAN

iUniverse

POWER OF DESTINY
POETRY

iUniverse books may be ordered through booksellers or by contacting:

iUniverse
1663 Liberty Drive
Bloomington, IN 47403
www.iuniverse.com
1-800-Authors (1-800-288-4677)

Because of the dynamic nature of the Internet, any web addresses or links contained in this book may have changed since publication and may no longer be valid. The views expressed in this work are solely those of the author and do not necessarily reflect the views of the publisher, and the publisher hereby disclaims any responsibility for them.

Any people depicted in stock imagery provided by Getty Images are models, and such images are being used for illustrative purposes only.
Certain stock imagery © Getty Images.

ISBN: 978-1-5320-8718-9 (sc)
ISBN: 978-1-5320-8717-2 (e)

Print information available on the last page.

iUniverse rev. date: 10/31/2019

POWER OF DESTINY

MY SALUTATION TO THEE OH DIVINE MOTHER GAYTRI
DEDICATED TO A WORLD OF PEACE
KARRAN P. DEOKARRAN (VICKRAM)

GAYTRI MANTRA

Om Bhur Bhuvaḥ Suvah
Tat-savitur Vareñyaṃ
Bhargo Devasya Dhīmahi
Dhiyo Yonaḥ Prachodayāt

General meaning: We meditate on that most adored Supreme Lord, the creator, whose effulgence (divine light) illumines all realms (physical, mental and spiritual). May this divine light illumine our intellect.

Word meaning: Om: The primeval sound; Bhur: the physical body/ physical realm; Bhuvah: the life force/the mental realm Suvah: the soul/ spiritual realm; Tat: That (God); Savitur: The Sun, Creator (source of all life); Vareñyam: adore; Bhargo: effulgence (divine light); Devasya: supreme Lord; Dhīmahi: meditate; Dhiyo: the intellect; Yo: May this light; Nah: our; Prachodayāt: illumine/inspiration

Knowledge is inherent in man, in the brain it resides
Like the body it need healthy food to survive
God so love man he creates a special food for the brain
It is called Gaytri mantra love and honesty it contains
Chant it night and day wherever you go or stay
Gaytri mantra will protect you every day
The mind become healthy the body pure
All material and spiritual illness it will cure
Oh man we came into this world for a short time
We will have to leave it is the will of the divine
Whatever we do now will determine our future
Chanting Gaytri Mantra your tomorrow will be brighter

God gives fruits and vegetable for the body to sustain
He gives Gaytri Mantra to feed the mind, soul and brain
Dishonesty, lust, passion, and hatred man began to cherish
God creation suffer, and his children had to punish

By Karran P. Deokarran July 2017 U.S.A

MY MESSAGE

My fellow Brothers and Sisters the world today that we live in have become corrupt, dishonest and evil but why, if there is a reason then there will be answers, the reasons for lust, anger, hatred and ego every one want to become rich materially to own as much cars many houses large bank account large amount of lands to maintain this principle there must be destruction to others but those who embark on this mission, have the ever gone to a funeral have they ever look into the coffin, then a careful look would reveal the following the coffin is too small to hold all that was acquire not even a pen in his hands to write another check so all the individual try to accumulate materially remain and he is gone then on the other hand God become angry with man actions and he sent Hurricane, Flooding, Earthquake, tsunami and so many more disaster which none of us can controlled so what is the answer, we must able to please God and help our fellow human by showing love be honest with each other be truthful and help each other the world will be a better place for all of us to live this I promise, to those who embark on a mission to make the most powerful weapon you must understand one thing for millions of years he that born must die so why waste money to build weapon to kill those who will die one day this one action makes our leaders and the intelligent sector the master of illiteracy, I can only hope and pray that someday the few half naked Human Hungry for real knowledge walking in silent will able to come forward and unmasked their true potential of the real Human race where Mother Earth can once again experience peace love and comfort when that time will arrive milk will be scattered upon the earth no more liquor and blood there will be peace love and honest behavior everywhere moral value will engulf every nation and truth will be the god on Earth when that time will come Man and animal will be friend, Oh man you are not this physical body of five elements you are a soul which is a spark of God accompanied by a spirit or guardian a subconscious mind that record the present actions and reveal the past actions and direct the mind to allowed those actions to be rewards which is called destiny the big secret is we are given an opportunity to correct what have happen in the past by practicing honesty love and truth this will ensure future birth will be reward with human dignity and to climb the ladder to greater height the practice of religion help to motivate the mind if it is practice with truth love and honesty or it can become dangerous if practice with hatred the big secret remain with the individual, mind comes from the subtle part of the food we eat there are two type of food created and two type of mind display movable and immovable if one eat immovable food the mind become stable and can be easily controlled if one eat movable food then the mind move faster than the wind think of a deer it power is it speed when one eat the deer the mind become fast like the deer this is the reason why one should live on vegetable and fruits finally I wish to advice that you practice and experience for yours

BIOGRAPHY

Born on the 31st March 1958 in a little village call bath Mahaicony in Guyana south America to the parents of Deokarran and Koomarie both my mom and dad had previous marriage my dad had a son name Lakeram and my mom had a daughter name Leela my mom and Dad together had four sons and two daughters I was the eldest of six my name was given as Karran according to the Hindu book followed by Dirjodhan, Mangal, Lalchand, Nandinee and Hemwantie our parents were very poor and fishing was the only means of lively hood, I being the eldest had little chance of going to school, at the age of twelve, I had to go with my father to catch fish and shrimp from mid night to next day 10am then from 12pm I will go to school at 4th standard I had to leave school my dad will always say son never give up, knowledge don't come from anywhere it is within seek god help and you will have the best of knowledge The unfolding story of my journey begin in January 1970 at the age of twelve I started the fishing career, early February my father ask me to plant the Holika plant (a Castrol plant) which will be burnt on the full moon night forty days from the day of the planting which will be followed by the celebration of Phagwa marking the beginning of the Hindu new year, the whole process involve fasting, feeding the plant every morning a piece of dried leaf and water Holika represent the wicked sister of an evil King who wanted to kill his son because he preach the name of God this was the beginning of my vegetarian life Holi is the destruction of evil and the protection of good this is how my father had wanted me to be on this sacred journey in this birth, my father teach me one word (Help) he said practice this and everything else you will get, after the separation of my mother and father in 1976 my mom migrate to Suriname my Brothers and Sisters went with her I remain with my father we abandon fishing I started to work in a rice mill doing laborer work, the same year 1976 I join the P.Y.O. the youth arm of the P.P.P. this was the beginning of my political mission and so I choose two path to carry out my mission to help mankind, Politic to help economic development and Religion for Spiritual development as I traverse this rough journey many things have happen my duty was to move ahead, in 1980 I married to Nalenine against the wishes of both side parents however it was approved by destiny because she was destine to help me in my journey she give birth to four, beautiful children namely Latchmi, Menakshi, Bhanmatie and Chuniram. The first real trial begin when I was kidnap on the 26 of April 1989 from my home and taken to some unknown place, it was menakshi first birthday two years later I would see her again, for six days I was kept in hiding been tortured without food and water place in a cell naked lying on a concrete floor that is always wet I was taken out on a regular routine blind folded and taken to some room I will be place on a chair then I would strap everything seems to be operating electrical then I will be shock with current the voltage constantly increase then something would place over my head and it will adjust squeezing my head until I lost consciousness I will be beaten on my back and chest, I will be hang by my foot in the air, then my head will be place in a toilet bowl and ice water flush on my head I would be question about the P.P.P. leaders planning to overthrow the Government I have already give up living and so I have no concern answering any question after six days I was taken to some unknown place pickup by another group taken to the police head quarter and later charge for treason taken to court and then to prison where I would spend 544days before I won my case and was release to be unite with my family some of the lawyers which play a very important role are Khemraj Ramjattan, Charls Ramson, Bernard DE Santos, Ralph Ramkarran, Moses Bhagwan, Amnesty international, and a few others lawyer whose name I cannot remember, the many Guyanese living in the U.S.A. protest at the U.N. headquarter in the U.S.A. all of whom I wish to thank for their support and the courage they give during the trial. After I was release, I continue political work with the P.P.P. many questions were asked and is still asking why the P.P.P. play a low profile after the treason case finish and continue to do the same those question will be answering sometime soon. I was one never like by many of the leading people in freedom house but was always close to Cheddi Jagan the leader of the party the reason was I always have a different interpretation of communism I always believe the Russian and Cuban were not communist but dictator and the opportunity for individual to move up was the most difficult task, I always believed that communism can be best describe by the Holy Ramayana and the rule of king Dasarath the father of lord Rama which is difficult to practice in this sinful age especially when truth, love, and honesty is lost the present communist system is design to help empower family and friend through a political system, on the other side the capitalist system allowed for exploitation of man by man this system will disappear over a period of time by then the world will be in poverty and both system will disappear, let examine the system not by name but by action those who say they are communist empowering minority meaning an executive body which make decision to control majority on the other hand those who practice capitalist system allowed minority to controlled wealth and majority to live in poverty the two system will clash one day like thunder and lighting and will vanish forever then a new system will born, a system where those empower to manage and those bless to secure wealth will work together to help the world of human live happily that system will be called humanism or Humanist Democracy, This my political belief the prison life is one of fate in yourself and the courage to stand the many trials and temptation it helps me to awaken the inner self to control the mind and to search for answers, after I was out of prison wining my case I continue with the P.P.P. I always criticize the party system after the win in 1992 and the party controlled the government the government decided to hold local government election which was a bold step toward the right direction I contest the wood land/farm N.D.C. on the P.P.P. ticket and we won 10 seat, the P.N.C. 8 seat I was elected the chairman my immediate task was to win the trust and confident of the opposition this was important if we are going to help people leaders of the P.P.P. we're not happy with me and many label me as P.N.C. however, my mission was to build a great N.D.C. the job was a voluntary, it was meant to give service to the people I spent twelve years at the helm of the N.D.C. and I enjoyed every single day helping people for Cheddi Jagan he always complements me for what I am doing but the rest hate me in the party executive in 2006 the P.P.P. won the election and Bharat Jagdeo was the President he had wanted me to become the region five chairman however the party executive did not like it and we settle for the vice chairman the chairman was given a third term of failure President Jagdeo have always proven that the system was wrong but he was helpless he was made a president by those who hold the power in the party and were always deem(we put you there do what we want) lives was miserable for him I had close contact with him many time he voice his concern he want to resign but I will encourage him to stay on being the vice chairman of region five I was assign chairman of the works committee it is a powerful committee in the region it an area where corruption can be protected or can be remove there were fear everywhere because everyone know I will put a stop to many of the wrong thing happening in the region my first day in office as I sit on my chair I pull a draw from the desk there I discover an envelope with a set of transport these transport belongs to persons who had applied for house lot from the Government and the transport were to be given to the applicant, and were never to be in the vice chairman office but all the names were people living abroad the rest is a long story I took the transport to the chairman office and give him he look at me and did not say a word I then change the works committee rules from the chairman of the committee making the decision to the committee making the decision and those decision approve at the region meeting that meeting is made up of Government and opposition members so fair play was put in place contractor were been paid promptly I don't keep any one document they are sent for payment immediately this is how I streamline all the area I was in charge, health was another area I had to change a number of things to get it working in 2010 there were two contractor with two roads of nine million dollars contract each, when the works was about 15% a certain minister want me to sign payment for 90% work I refuse I was threaten by the contractor but that did not turn me I was offer two million I refuse then I wrote the incidence at the back of the voucher and leave it on my desk before leaving the office on the 24th December 2010 for a two month vacation in the united states of America no one know I was leaving for America and that I had a permanent visa I leave Guyana on the 26 December 2010 as I step on the plane step I look at Guyana with tears in my eyes and folded hands I silently wish my country a better future because my return would be long I wrote my resignation and leave it with eldest daughter who did not manage to get her visa, corruption was the main reason for me to decide to leave Guyana my commitment to

Guyana and its people are deep down in my heart my life was at stakes when minister want me to get into corruption who will protect me in the fight against corruption Although I am living in America my mind always with the Guyanese, because of this love I begin a spiritual search to find an answer to the real problem in Guyana which I wrote in a few beautiful verses title (50 years of pain and struggle) it is the answer to Guyana problem a final sacrifice I am prepared to make, No Government can settle in Guyana peaceful the slaves and indenture labor came with spiritual power no one ever show respect for their soul and spirit we have to understand that as human beings, we are not this body which is made up of five element we are souls and spirits with great powers and can do great things even when we leave this body unless certain act are carried out for the soul and spirit by those who remain in the human body priority for those action begin with the close relative these action is important for the continuation of the human existence it doesn't matter how educated, how smart or how honest one is as soon he or she get into public office a spiritual force is there to take care of you, such power will always miss lead you unless you can satisfy its need if one should take a careful look at the things happening at the mandir (KALI) if one take a careful look at the behavior of the pujari or priest and his follower one can understand the power of the spirit pretending to be holy giving themselves name of holy people unless one can live a holy life how can the incarnation of god speak through these people who do not live a righteous life all of this had happen because we were not living a righteous life these spirit take controlled of our body and do all crazy things I go through many trials and am saying what I have experience in this life to learn the secret I had to get involve here is where country and people have find themselves in problem any one can sit in one of these mandir just pay careful attention to the language of the pujari when the spirit would speak through them you will quickly understand what is happening in this world to combat such situation it takes one to undertake great sacrifice honesty in everything love for the world truth the watch word believe in God every religion must be seen as a part of the almighty we must able to remove from our heart distrust, hatred, lust, greed and egoism pay respect for our fore parents who made great sacrifice who work as slave and indenture labor for the good of their off spring I urge every Guyanese to pay tribute to our fore parent crime and corruption will over and a great nation will take birth in this world, I always believe that every nation have the right to determine their own path of development my reason is every nation have their own culture, some have their own language their natural resource will be different and so their development strategy will be different there is only one nation on earth which have all the natural resource the whole world might have and don't have a development strategy after fifty years of independence is the country of my birth Guyana in south America, a country of millions of acre of land and it citizens have a problem getting a house lot to build a house to live in or an acre of land to plant food to survive. Every government elected to office spend their first two year searching to see what the previous Government did the next two year is to find ways and means to help family and friends and to secure for themselves the last year is to prepare for the next election and how much promise would be made to win another five year term, Guyana have a population of five hundred thousand people with some of the most brilliant minds some of the most skillful farmers and yet we are the second poorest nation in the world, what a great joke in a land of the great political jokers, I came to the U.S.A. to learn what is America and why everyone coming to America what I found what the politician doing in my country Guyana the people are allowed to do it in the U.S.A. the freedom to become rich materially, but I search to find moral value, cultural value religious value in practice have all disappear what I found growing very fast is hatred, lust, anger. Crime and corruption the long term result is destruction of man by man all I can do is to hope and pray that a few good men will remain to start a new generation after god will put an end to all the wrong on earth, my fellow Brothers and Sisters, Mothers and Fathers it is our moral obligation to preserve the human race even if it is one percent all it take is a little practice of honesty, love be truthful to whatever you do try to help your fellow human believe that there is a god above looking at everything we do when we leave this body we take nothing with us we should protect nature, we must not want to kill the cow for food which take care of us from a baby to old age by giving us milk to live strong and healthy this we must preserved this is the biggest sin we are committing as human I only hope

xvi

and pray that my message will help in some way to change the mind of man every Poem is a message from the heart from the inner selves something I do not want to keep for myself read and cherish God blessing be with everyone no matter which religion you belong to, God is one he take different form to please different nation.

Living in the United State of America was a very good experience I first came to Orlando Florida with my wife and children except for my eldest daughter Latchmi had to stay back in Guyana the second one Menakshi marry and live in New York I found a job at West Gate Resort a very good job the company very professional I love the job after three months destiny say it's time to leave who am I to dictate Family problem become the medium and so I leave the job and move to New York it take two months to find a job my daughter father in law working at a ware house in long island get me a job it's the hardest work I would do in this life with little pay I had to do it to take care of the family only pay bills I meet People from all over the world, I talk to many of them I learn from them the many problems they face in their country these many conversation lead to start search for answers to the many problems I prayed to Mother Sarasvati seeking divine inspiration which I used to publish my first Book name A Message from the Inner self it wasn't a success so I continue my second book was poetry Power of the Mind this time it was on the market with some response this prompt me to continue this time I want to tell the World that all is not lost I have learn many things in the U.S.A. I do not intend to live here all my life but to go back to Guyana my promise to free the Guyanese people I will always keep, The politic like every other country there is problem in the U.S.A. outside the U.SA there is one story about the U.S.A. and it imperialist policy and in such society Government don't help people this was always the story in Guyana but it was totally different when I decided to live it a person not working in the U.S. get help from the Government Unemployment, food stamp free house to live in free medical and I am sure places like Russia, China and many more countries have big business middle class and poor people but here is the problem, two words Communism and Capitalism with no real meaning behind them Communism cannot be achieved in this sinful age it entail Truth Honesty and love it entail Government manage the affairs of the country provide cheap or free service using state revenue one the other hand Capitalism is a dream any one can become rich as long as you can work save and invest, I can tell you thousands of Guyanese who borrow money to go to America work save bring their family and can go home back as millionaire those who left behind are still in poverty no country is perfect and will never be perfect as long as the lust for power and position continue to flourish.

To my four children Latchmi, Menakshi, Bhanmatie and chuniram this is all I can give you the greatest treasure of my life knowledge bless by God to my four grandson Aryan, Davin, Chitanand, Vahin and kavin I love you to my heart preserved your grandfather legacy your world will be a great one, To my three son-in law Satash, Parsram and Surendra knowledge is sacred it help you to preform good action which is the only thing one carry after death to all my family, friends and peace loving children of mother Earth the only thing I have to offer is Truth, Love and Honesty always remember God is watching you from above do good love each other even in poverty the rich and the poor they all meet in the burial ground to the world of evil doer please remember history teach us Truth and good deeds always triumph over evil so give up your taught, I pay special homage to Vedanta Acharya Pt Mahendranauth Doobay a highly qualified Hindu Priest and spiritual leader from Guyana and living in the U.S.A. he is a frequent visitor to India, he meet with Shree Satya Sai Baba before Baba pass away Pandit always preach that he is making every possible effort to spread the truth of Hinduism I learn many things from him and without any doubt I can testify that in the heart of Pt Doobay I have found some good quality, he wanted to help humanity.

MY PRAYER

My salutation to thee oh mom and dad
Thank you for bringing me into this world Thank you
for teaching me to walk the path of righteousness
And to worship the almighty god for happiness
My humble salutation to thee oh Supreme God
For creating and preserving this universe
Give me an opportunity to experience your creation
Give me knowledge and wisdom so I can find salvation
Give me a chance to love and served you with devotion
Give me courage to stand the many trials and temptation
Bless me with the will to served others
Bless me so when I leave this body, I will be with your forever
Oh, supreme god I bow to you in all thy form and glory
Shower your love and admiration upon all too live happy
Oh my god if there is anything you wish to bless me with
Let it be thy will that I never live to regret
Let from birth to birth I experience your greatness and
understand your creation which can give real happiness
Give me health and strength to chant the glory of your name
Let the tears from my eyes fill your heart with love oh divine

CONTENTS

100 BIRTH ANNIVARSARY

5th November 1917 a great son was Born in my family
To Maria and Attoi my Grand Parents they rejoice happily
He was the second out of thirteen children a bright star
His Father an Alcoholic his Mother a religious acetic with great care
Hindu tradition the Priest give his name as Deokarran
He came with a message help each other oh Man
Born in a Hindu home he shares the love of Christianity
A nonalcoholic and vegetarian he lives a life of purity
Seventy-six years he spent in the human body
Singing the name of God his closest company
Helping other was his dedicated and only mission
Practicing his religion was his greatest possession
He became the father of seven loving children
He ensures great care was given to them
He preaches God is the giver of everything
Whoever believe in him will get his blessing
This great religious icon happens to be my Father
With my Mother Koomarie they live happy together
Then destiny said it's time to fulfill past desire
A separation become possible for the future

My Father always say seek the divine blessing
Practice honesty to you great knowledge belongs
The only good you can do is to help others
This evil age it hard to understand your own Brother

People call him sadoo because of his yoga practice
He is full of love and patient and bear no malice
Faith first trial his Brother and Sister his enemy
Show no hatred it is call destiny Always
Then one evening he sits with his two grand Asha and Usha
In a loving voice like a holy prayer he said live happily

I am going to see what was created by God almighty
Then he said son do good you will have a great family
The next morning, he is gone his body remain lifeless
He said never mourn for me I must take my test
His body became ashes but the name Deokarran is fame
He always says walk the path of riotousness in my name
My salutation to thee oh Divine creator
For giving me such a sincere and loving Mother and Father
Their love and affection will full fill my mission
Dad your life and works my inspiration

THE COW MY MOTHER

The cow will always be care and love as my Mother
She gives me milk, Ghee, Cheese, Paneer and Butter She
gives love, strength good health and a bright future
Why would anyone kill her for their supper?

The cow so peaceful honest and loving
Oh Man live like the cow and learn to be caring
She eats grass, leaves and drink water
She feed her young give to others she never sees a doctor

The cow has no policeman court or lawyer but live happy
Her urine and waste fertile the plants to grow healthy
The cow display maturity, love, and purity
She is a great Mother, caring and trustworthy
Oh Man learn to live and love from the cow
Show respect and care no harm should be allow
Let her live-in comfort and always be happy
She will give you milk to feed you and your family

A LESSON FOR MANKIND

Some call it hurricane sandy
Some say it was powerful and windy
Some say it was Mother Nature at work
Some say it is the wind God, why only some get hurt
Whatever had happened and whatever everyone says
It was a lesson for everyone to learn in a day
Man must not boast about power
God the almighty can strike at any hour
There are nuclear missiles every where
A small hurricane came, everyone get fear
This is another message God send
Oh, man do good and stop pretend
We must stop hurting each other
Follow the rules of our scripture
Stop boast about who is powerful
Who alive, to their good deeds there should be thankful?
Oh man the time is coming and coming very past
The earth burden not long more it will last
Repent now oh man or thou shall punish
Everything the eyes can see will vanish
Earthquake, Hurricane, Flooding are only warning
These are lesson for man to change their evil thinking
Those who refuse the Almighty warning
Will live to see real material suffering

FIFTY YEARS OF PAIN AND STRUGGLE

They were brought from far away Africa
To slave in Beautiful Guyana
They were brought from far away India
To labored in Beautiful Guyana

Time have destroyed their identity
Their culture and tradition were lost in history
Their language was compromise by their slave master
Their Religion was sacrifice for schooling which was a disaster

Cuffy and Damon wage a battle for freedom
The Indian selfishness were held at ransom
Jagan and Burnham continue the struggle
Unity play a great role, freedom became possible
Then came the 26 of May 1966 bright like a star
The cries of a Nation turn into joy near and far
The struggle of our fore parent was forgotten
50 years later their sacrifice become the Nation burden
as we hoist the golden Arrowhead for the 50th time
No amount of speeches and promises can remove their pains
Oh, leaders I humbly ask that you seek the divine intervention
Ask for forgiveness and give our fore parent salvation

Dancing on the street is only more molestation
The fighting spirit of our ancestor need salvation
No Government will find peace in my Beautiful Guyana
Unless we join hands together to liberate our ancestor

The tears of our ancestor only brought flood each year
Their anger brought drought and fear
Their love keeps the nation existing but in poverty
Their roaming spirit must be liberated to bring unity

DON'T EAT MEAT

Animals were created to do everything like man
Hatred started when killing for food began
Animal have no Judge, Jury or policeman
They roam the forest freely like everyone
Man said they are civilized they can think well
They build bombs and missiles to send everyone to hell
They first eat all the animal then removed all the trees
Then boost they have knowledge god give them free
Man is looking to blame someone for nature destruction
In their search, they create among each other more confusion
Man, first try to replace God and become the new creator
Now they fail and will be the greatest destroyer
God will soon build another Arc to save his creation
Flood and fire everyone will see his power of destruction
God did it once everyone preaching none doing the listening.
He will do it again, so humans will learn the right thing

A LONE TRAVELER

A lone traveler I am searching for peace
Everywhere I go the voice of hatred increase
IT fascinating to see how man destroying themselves
Grabbing at illusion which will never help thee
If one goes to Arabia pay homage to Allah
If one goes to India pay homage to lord Rama
If one goes to Israel pay homage to Lord Jesus
If you go to America all it wanted is your praises
Every time I try to say of my God
I am disturbed by a missile going off loud and hard
Every time I try to shout Peace
The news is the death toll increase
God create this world a beautiful place
Oh man your action is a disgrace
You become blind you kill your Brothers and Sisters
Your action is like that of a monster
Oh, Mother of the ocean come wash this land
Oh, Father of the Air destroy those evil hands
Oh, mighty sun burns the evil
Oh, creator let peace and love prevail

A MEMORABLE THANK YOU

They saw land they were dying from cold and need shelter
The Native Americans welcome them as their brother
They were given wine and Turkey to quench their hunger
Then Friday morning they start to slaughter
They were not deemed terrorist, immigrant or invader
They were given the status of explorer and occupier
The Indian resistance was a long-fought battle
They were defeated and given the waste land to settle
The Indian lost the battle because they were not fighter
They were peace loving children of the creator
Their tears and blood were scattered upon their sacred soil
They are the true sons and Daughter of America
These Native Indian live happy for thousands of years
Until lust and ego came to take what their share
Until this day such an act is celebrated with pomp and joy
Only the native Indian in their heart loud their cry
On this Thanksgiving Day, I salute you oh Native Indian
Your bravery and loyalty will be remembered by Historian
History tells us that truth and honesty is part of the creator
Patient and time are all its take for such divine answer

By Karran P. Deokarran 11/22/2016 U.S.A.

DEATH

Time is moving very fast do what you must, quick Why are
you weeping, lets sing and dance, life has no trick?
Everyone came for a purpose they design their own journey
This body we lament over will return slowly
Oh, death if you come for me while sleeping Don't wake
me just hold my hands together, we are going
Just a short stop to say hello to friends and family
We shall then continue this long journey
There must be no regret when I leave this body
But to say thanks, mission accomplish, and I am ready
These two beautiful hands I used to help other Thanks
to my two feet you took me across rough waters
Empty hands I wave goodbye sisters and brothers
Follow the path of wise men, we will reach together
House, car and bank account, they are not going
The judge and jury are ready for my hearing
At birth, I pledge to use this body none must get hurt
I promise to hold other hands and walk until I depart
My smiling face must not change your weeping eyes
I came alone, and I am leaving all alone goodbye

DON'T FIGHT DESTINY

Destiny is never about what we want while in this body
It's all about what we must do, and we must ready
Many years ago, while working to make others' lives happy
To America you and your family must leave immediately

On the plane step I stood and wave Guyana goodbye
It my home, my country, my people I cried
For five hour I sit in the air a million thoughts why
I step out at Miami airport touch the soil again I cry

As I settle down a voice came singing
My son not to this place you belong
You will have to move on another journey
Great opportunity awaits you it's your destiny

On the shores of New York, I decided to settle
I found a job to take care of my financial needs a little
A trembling voice revel many stories
With my pen and paper, I reveal great memories

The American dream came smiling before me
A poet and an author this my gift to thee
Learn as much as you can my child without fear
Your next gift when you become a citizen here

The American flag I shall always honored and respect
Great opportunities lie ahead no one will regret
Thank you oh America for the opportunity I was given
Thank you for giving so many nations a haven

Whatever wrong one might have done it destiny at work
Who are we to decided who get help and who get hurt
Everything the eyes can see will vanish nothing will remain It
happen before it will happen now, and it will happen again

By Karran P Deokarran N.Y. U.S.A. 08/23/2016

FIDEL CASTRO GONE

Like every other Human he came into this world
He did his job and left his name printed in gold
Those who did nothing will always remember Castro
A whole life they wasted looking at his show Some call
him a Dictator the Cuban call him their God father
His heart was for the poor and helpless everywhere
The wicked see in him everything evil and bad
The good man accepts his help and cheer him happy and glad
He was a human he did great for his people and country
His enemy call him the world greatest tyranny
He gives health care to the world for people to live happy His
country was poor, but exploitation was never his priority
History will judge Fidel for the many things he has done
Be it good or bad he did it for everyone
He executes his duty with dignity, pride and satisfaction
He gives to many helps for economic salvation
Great minds do not see something call death
They admire one duty and leave this body without regret
Fidel will be remembered for many things he left behind You
live your live what you sow you will reap it God design.

ELECTION U.S.A. 2016

One year of intense campaign in sun and rain
Hillary and Trump telling the nation what they will gain
Promise and promise everywhere of all kind
Talking to a nation that is politically blind

The campaign was never about which leader have the ability
Words of insult was trading every day on each other integrity
Confusion was building high on a nation living on hope
Every leader talking donation none talk of salvation

Then came election day in a nation that preach democracy the
result will determine what happen to people and country
As the result start to flow tense moment were everywhere
Some jumping for joyed others expressing fears'
The nation cast their vote Hillary secure a majority
The democratic system says Trump the winner with a minority
The result was determined by an electoral college
A system develops without any real knowledge and so,
this great nation will get a government they deserve
A nation with a dream will remain undisturbed Like and
dislike will never build nation and develop country
Moral value will be destroyed none will be happy

FOOTPRINT

My footprint will only have value and befit time
When I can follow the path of great men of divine
The footprint of the wise was mark with loyalty
These prints were left behind with Truth, Love and Honesty

These prints were left on the platter of a white lily
The path of kindness is rigged but sweet and lovely
Thorns become soft when these prints are left with a smile
Walk these paths in the name of god just for a while

The illusive world always tries to erase these prints
These prints are nourished by rain drops and sun lights
These prints shine like diamonds and glitter like gold
These prints set great example and never grow old

My missions are to walk the path of wise men left behind
To be honest, loyal, sincere and to help mankind
This one gift I seek from thee of God Almighty
Bless my footstep with love and divinity

By Karran P. Deokarran [Vickram]

GOD OR RELIGION

God is the Almighty a force that dwell in and around everyone
Those who recognized him to pleased them he took a form God
is so gracious you get what you want if ask with sincerity
No one go empty hand he is all merciful and divinity
Religion made by man to quench the thirst of man ego within
Books were written songs were sung many names were given
Weapon were made wars were created all in some god name
To give a helping hand none cares all in search of fame
None believer calls the name God more than those praying
Seated in one heart is the divine ready to help without asking
Church going is convenient and on a secret mission Helping
nature and God creation should be man real passion
So how best can one attempt to describe God Almighty
Love, Patient, Truth, Honesty Practice with dignity
Moral value the steppingstone to achieve great success
Religion or God, a peace of mind will bring progress

By Karran Deokarran 01/ 06/2017 U.S.A.

GUYANA OH LOVELY GUYANA

Oh, lovely Guyana you are my soul my heart my everything
Your sweet voice I can hear far away keep calling
Your gold and diamond glittering in the morning sun
And the lovely parrot singing with joy to its satisfaction
Oh, Guyana your abundance of water and rich fertile land
You can remove the world of hunger and feed mankind
Time is moving fast oh lovely Guyana you must awake
50yrs' you were sleeping your people you forsake
Oh, lovely Guyana the tears and pain of your children unbearable
Wake up wake up your dignity and moral value is redeemable
You were born from tyranny a conquer a slave master
Your children the offspring of two great nation need a future
Oh, lovely Guyana your children pride their hospitality
They came from great culture with religious dignity
They were born out of indenture labor and slavery
They deserved to live in freedom together happily

Karran P. Deokarran 03/10/2017

GUYANA WILL BE FAMOUS

The Dutch make Guyana a country famous and wealthy
Producing cotton for clothing is thinking Humanity
They were hardworking, and ambitious set of people
Their technology great their money was gold unbelievable

Then came the British beat the Dutch and chase them away
Very lazy they brought the African to work without pay
Their mission to find the Dutch gold searching everyday
The Dutch honesty is protecting it wherever it lays

Then God decided to put a stop to British slave expansion
He sends two brave men to represent their clan
Jagan and Burnham fight the British for freedom
History will worship them Guyana have won

Then began the fight for power and position
Hatred and lust destroy a hard-working nation
We did not pay homage to the Dutch for their country
Guyana will be a rich country with lovely people in history
Thanks to Burnham and Jagan who started the mission
Their leadership lack moral value they had no solution
Guyanese still can't understand their true position
Leaving wealth and happiness and choose migration

Oh, my beautiful Guyana on day you will be great again
When all the coward is gone wisdom and love will born
One day the Dutch People will be given true liberation
Then Guyana will be flourish as a great and prosperous nation

The spirit of our four parents will ascend to higher plain
Oh, Guyana you will be history once again
All I ask for is honesty, truth, unity and love
All divine guidance will come from above

By Karran Deokarran

17

HAPPY NEW YEAR

With folded hands, oh God I bow to thee Let
this New Year morning bring happiness to me
Whatever had happened in my life yesterday
Will make me stronger today
As I look through my window the sun shining bright
And the cool wind blowing through the morning light
The whispering of birds can be heard everywhere
The sound of happy New Year fills the year

I took a cool bath to refresh myself
Then I kneel before my alter the home of my life
I lite a light to remove all darkness
I bow to thee oh God lead me the path of goodness
Oh man you are not this body you are a spiritual might
Do not stuff this body with waste it is not right
Your battle is against lust and hatred you must fight
This body to dust it will return prepare your flight
On this day I renew my old vow which I do every year
Action thy duty reward not thy concern that which I care
I will dedicate my life for a better life for mankind
Oh man be honest and loving your life will be different

A JOURNEY BACK TO GUYANA

It was an amazing trip back to my homeland
Everything looks so wonderful its nature command
Drinking coconut and cane juice every morning
Enjoying the hot sun and cool wind was exiting

Everyone would say enjoyed your vacation
My reply I am here to preform religious function
It is telling my mother land I love you always
Thank God to keep you safe and happy all day

Back home many are crying thing bad
Drinking alcohol, smoking tobacco they are happy and glad
Many complain the government doing nothing
Yet they wanted bigger road too many cars running

The vegetable and fruits are so tasty and fresh
This make Guyana the greatest and the best
No one will never go hungry in my lovely Guyana
No wars but great adventure for every foreigner

By Karran P. Deokarran 05/01/2017 U.S.A.

WOMEN FOR WHITE HOUSE

Me America you America
Come on everybody we are marching with Hilary
Hilary a woman with integrity
Hilary wanted to end poverty

Hilary a leader with great ability
Hilary wanted real unity
Give her a chance to prove her quality
Vote Hilary for the presidency

Many try to defame her integrity
They are searching her email for love story
She is fighting for young and old equally
She will ensure everyone live happily

So, come everyone unite together
Hillary our Mother Hillary our future
Hillary, she is talking of building nation
Other talking of war with the Asian

Hillary talking of good education
Other talking Obama care destruction
So, people listen and listen carefully
We are voting for Hillary

Hillary, she is talking of wage increase
Other are talking of immigrant decrease
Hillary, she is talking of job creation
Other talking of religious destruction
So, if you want love and unity in your country
Then give Hillary the Presidency

Karran P, Deokarran 03/05/201

DRINKING ALCOHOL

If drinking alcohol and smoking tobacco
Give happiness and self-satisfaction which is slow death
Then drinking poison will bring greater happiness
And self-renunciation

GIFT

Everyone born in this world came with two gifts
A bag of tools and a book of rules
Which can make our lives good and pure

PRAYER

Prayers are the Awakening of the conscience
The more silent it is being recited
The greater effect it carries
Try it every morning and be happy

FLOWERS

The flowers give its fragrance to all
The flowers give nectar for the bees
The bees give honey for everyone
Human give Hatred, Passion and Anger
And look for money, car, house and power

THE POLITICAL GAME

Democracy is the cause of trust and distrust in the politic
Democracy say majority is superior over minority, the tricks
Democracy a tool to secure political power for a few
Democracy a propaganda network, you lie to get through

The game must have two main political parties
Both with the same agenda it started back in the forties
The motive is to control a nation wealth and hold power
This game was played for long and is about to over

The planner never stops work a new game in the making
Independence like a rising star everywhere singing
The rich and educated on the front line doing the planning
The poor and helpless are being used to do protesting

This new political system will not last very long
Poverty will breed criminals and they will grow strong
The rich will be destroyed the poor will die of hunger God
will help the few good ones who know he is the creator

By Karran Deokarran 08/12/2017 U.S.A

IN SEARCH FOR PEACE

Each morning as I look at the rising of the sun
My heart keeps asking would peace ever won
With Guns Bombs and missiles every where
Oh lord even the maker now living in fear

Lust for wealth breads Anger, Hatred and passion
For power and position killing become a condition
Give me the courage and the will to find answers
So that the pain in my heart will gone forever

The United Nation was formed to unite Countries
Rich nation took advantage and called it Democracy
The commonwealth was formed to help depress nations
Communism and Capitalism the magic words for frustrations

Then came the None Aligned Movement a new trick
All that happen the poor countries continue to get kick
Then Destiny decided to make the final decision
Rich and poor either in the burial ground or cremation
So, the search for peace is over don't trust politician
Fill your heart with righteousness, love and devotion
Oh man every soldier is your sons and daughters
Tell them you want peace stop fighting each other

As I look at the beautiful sun fading fast away forever
A voice saying son give my message to every leader
Take warning seriously and stop pretending in the
form of Earthquake, and Hurricane I am coming

By Karran P. Deokarran (Vickram) 06/10/2017 U.S.A.

THREE BRANCHES OF A GOVERNMENT

Every Government is made up of three branches
The people or the law real power entrenches
The executive branches by the people is elected
The administrative branch by the executive selected

The executive agrees to manage the people affairs
The people affairs at an election they share
Agreements was reach and seal by the ballot
When the executive does otherwise kick them out

A united people the greatest power in a country
The executive branches exercise the people authority
The administrative branch must work without corruption
The people power creates a great nation

My message to all you great people of every nation
Blame not the executive, you are the solution
You cast your vote to elect the executive
When they fail, you must give new directive

By Karran P. Deokarran 05 /14

MIND

The human mind is the most powerful weapon
Feed it with love and honesty
It will be strong and healthy
Feed it with hatred and corruption
Watch how you embrace destruction

VEGETARIAN

Vegetable was created for man to eat and be strong
Fish was created to clean the earth of all waste
Animal was created to guard the forest and to be man friend

HERBS

Marijuana a herb created by God to cure all human illness
It was never meant to burn and smoke the brain
God, want you to drink it so a healthy body you will maintain

BE CAREFUL

Above the sky dwells our supreme father
He watches over all our behavior
Below our feet lies our dear Mother
She bears all our evil deeds without a whisper

By Karran Deokarran

THE EARTH

The earth bears it burden of evil without a whisper
Oh, man why harbor lust and anger
When your existence depends on the Creator
By Karran Deokarran

DUTY OF A CHILD

The duty of a child is to worship their Mother and Father
Bow with respect to their teacher
Then bow to God the Almighty creator

PERSONAL FAME

Those who strive only for personal fame
None will ever remember their name
A man who works all his life to help other
By the world, he will always be remembered Border
Mother earth bear the burden of all
Be it Good and evil for help she never call
Oh, man why become angry with others When you
are a mere drop in the ocean of the creator

THE WORLD OF EVIL

It is easier to find diamond and gold
Than to find someone to help their fellow man
If you want to own the world
Have faith in lies
If you want to be a shareholder in heaven
Have faith in truth and honesty
By Karran Deokarran

AWAKE

Awake arise oh son of Almighty God
Too long you have been sleeping
You are the store house of knowledge
In you lies the invincible power.to make the world better
By Karran Deokarran

HONESTY

Only if man can practice love and honesty
They will able to discover morality
The world can then benefit from their loyalty
The worship of women is the embodiment of dignity

WORKERS

Workers are those who fulfill assignment
Their thought and mind are to get the work done
Laborer are those who present for work
But always hide their presence in the work

TERRORIST

Terrorist are those who believe in destruction
Stay far away from them their mind is frustration
They will become none existence out of corruption
Terrorism is not guns and sword but bad administration

Politician are those who like to do plenty talking
But lack the knowledge to command any listening
Politician always believed their duty is to give order.
And listener have no right to question their behavior

WHAT TO DO

Do not try to do things to build number
Try to do things so that others will remember
Don't try to own the whole world of material things
Search first to find your soul and where it belongs

MAN, AND GOD

Man, can only proposed God decide and disposed
Dream can make man confused and misleading Reality
remove suspicion and give the mind satisfaction
Follow your destiny without complaint is your reward.

RESPECT

Always show respect to all living creature
Everything was created by the same creator
To destroy anything is to destroy the creator wishes
Help protect creation is the greatest of respect

MORAL VALUE

Morality make a nation great and prosperous
Loose it and patiently destruction awaits
Corruption, Crime economic failure is inevitable
Negative attitude will influence administrative behavior

DESTINY

Man, is the architect of his own destruction
He always keeps grabbing at material things
He forgets that to the creator everything belongs
And that the burial ground has no place for any thing

MANAGER

A perfect manager is a great leader
He explores the true ability of his worker
A good manager is one who manage for success
A manager is one who hold a position
But his problem he can't make decision.

A POWERFUL FORCE

Look through your window
With a smile ask your self
Who control the sun, the moon?
And The cool wind
Where they come from and where
They are going.

WHAT IS REAL HAPPINESS

If drinking alcohol and smoking
Tobacco brings happiness an
Self-satisfaction
Then drinking poison will bring greater
Happiness and self-renunciation

MAN BEHAVIOUR

Man were blessed to live and love each other
Never to live like lion and tiger
Fighting and killing each other

A UNIVERSITY

Oh, man this world in a university
Earn all the knowledge you seek lovingly
Nature your greatest lecture
Follow his teaching unfold your future

OH MAN

Oh Man you are great You are all powerful
Live a true life eat the right food Explore your real identity

LEADERS

Leaders are not commodity which can be manufactured
They are born out of a lineage of honesty Truth and love

BE CAREFUL

Oh Man be careful of your fellow Human
Who dress in all type of religious garbs
Exploiting your sympathy
To acquire wealth and fame

MOTHER EARTH

Birth and death come because of desire and action
Geeta say Karma the Bible say what you sow you shall reap
Finally, it is call destiny the most powerful ruler
Whatever action we preform must bear fruit
The only thing God do for us ensure our reward

By Karran Deokarran

MAN, OR A FLOWER

Flowers are regarded as very sacred, what they bring
Beautiful fragrance for all and nectar as blessing
The flower never asks the bees for any return
But ask the air to spread it fragrance every where

Man is regarded the greatest of all beings
They came with two gifts their greatest blessings
One is a bag full of tools to use with compassion
The other is a book of rules with righteous injunction

Man become lust for material thing
They abused his bag of tool and ruin his upbringing
His book of rules was hidden and a new one written
Man, action became very low and unforgiven

The flower fragrance and nectar with love was given
For man to evade others their book of rules was hidden
Hatred, Passion, Lust and anger become man lover
Beauty, love and compassion the greatness of the flower

By Karran Deokarran

A MOTHER LOVE

Today everyone with a kind heart saying happy Mother's Day
The evil minds show no care, have nothing to repay
The wise man worshipped his mother every day
This poor broken heart beggar mom gone far away

On this mother day, I come to you oh God with folded hands
Give me the courage to respect every mother my demand A
Mother courage love and dedication oh God is the greatest
To embrace that mother love is man greatest test

When we wake, and start crying in the middle of the night
Only mom is there to take care of me and sleep me right
When we grow up to be strong and healthy
We drink alcohol drunk kick our mother and be happy

This my message to all you children your mother is your god
Care her love her make her happy and glad
When your chapter will be written on the pages of history
Mothers love Mother love will be the main story

MY SALUTATION OH GOD

With folded hands I bowed to thee oh almighty
Creator, Proctor and Destroyer of Humanity
Guide me in all my words and action
So, I can lead a good life and attain salvation

Oh, merciful God bless me with knowledge and wisdom
Bless me so I can return to your kingdom
Bless my hands to help others as I walk this universe
Let my feet on the righteous path traverse

Bless me to share your love and affection
Bless all my taught and deeds with perfection
Bless me so that I never part from truth and honesty
This one gift I seek from thee oh Almighty

Thank you oh God for sending me on earth
Let me fulfil my destiny before I depart
Help me to take of this body you give me
And journey back to eternity

By Karran Deokarran 31/03/2017

A WISPER

I am Earth I am entrusted with all you lovely people prosperity
All I wanted is to give you everything to make you happy
All I ask you to hold each other hands and walk gently
You choose to walk alone your problem I look on silently

I am the Sun I have the power to give you energy
All I wanted is for you to be united and live lovingly
You dug up all the poison and let them in the air
You are the cause why your whole existence in fear

I am the Moon you always say I run till day catch me
Without me a healthy life is difficult for you to see
If you stay together your existence will be safer
So, decide oh man if you want to be happy or suffer

The creator assigns us to help you only if you will stay together
You choose your own path you can face great disaster
You refuse the creator and profess to be your own master You
give wars I give earthquake and, hurricane a reminder

By Karran Deokarran 01/01/2017 U.S.A.

MY STORY

From a poor humbly, family I was born
Fishing my first job for a daily bread to earn
I was only twelve years catching fish without fear
It was karma [past action] who cares

In pouring rain and the dark of the night
With water to my neck this my plight
Staying by my father side I care nothing
Only thinking of an honest living

Schooling I know I will be lost forever
Every day father would say help others
Surrender yourself to the feet of the almighty
He will bless you with knowledge for eternity

From a fisherman to a laborer
Then a carpenter and then a farmer
Then a politician and to a social worker
Then to an administer and to a secret admirer

Poverty makes many demands
Everywhere I go I try to give a helping hand
Those who lust for position see me their enemy
Sacrifice for others make me happy

None will carry their wealth to their grave
Many obstacles I had to brave
From righteousness I will never part
Until from this body I depart

By Karran Deokarran

A GREAT DEVOTEE

He came from a humble community in Guyana
He later migrates to the United States of America
From there destiny took him to his Mother land India
On his return he was carrying the flag of Hindu Dharma
Wherever he goes large crowd will follow to hear scripter
His melodious voice would charm his listener
He sings to his heart song of devotion
He earns great respect and international recognition
His return to Guyana saws the revival of Hindu Dharma
Large crowd will assemble to hear him at (Function) yajna
This great preacher has won millions of righteous hearts
His lesson was beware of illusion we will have to depart
This messenger and I become close friend while on his mission
His message was honesty, love and devotion
Then one day the supreme God said son time to come home
The great Prakash Gossai was travelling all alone
As he waves goodbye to his followers
You will always be my Sisters and Brothers
Do not leave the path of Religious scripture
Practice love and unity and live together

THE RISE OF BHARAT MATA

The people of the Bharat Mata (India) has finally awaken
The foundation of the Nehru dynasty has been broken
A leader was born to lead the nation to freedom
No more will anyone allowed to hold the Indian at Ransom

From a humble street corner tea seller in Gujrat India
He rises to the world greatest democracy leader
He preaches to his people honesty, love and sincerity
Progress his friend and corruption his enemy

His name is Narendra Modi a son of Bharat Mata
At his Mother feet he bows as India next Leader
He looks at the rising sun and bow with a smile
He worshipped Ganga Mata as a poor humble child

This humble son believes in peace and progress
His silence always put the enemy mind to test
His inauguration is one politician will remember
His invitees are those who will work for a bright future
And so, the World is about to witness another great change
The once mighty India will move to world highest stage
Fear have already start to linger in many evil minds
Because Modi first act was to seek guidance from the divine

The people of India deserve to regain their pride and glory
And in modi they put their thrust to make history
Time alone can answer all mankind problems in this World
The Indian have proven that the new era is about to unfold

My advice to you Brothers and Sisters of India
You have chosen a leader prepare your future
Your only pride is Bharat Mata [India] history
Your culture, your religion, your unity is your prosperity

By Karran Deokarran

175 YEARS AGO

They sail across the black sea
No one know what their future will be
They were fool to come to Guyana
They were told their work will be to sift sugar

This is the British message 175 years ago
In India among the coolie bubo
Then they sail the Indian to a land call Guyana
To work on the sugar plantation, with great exploitation

They were told they will be paid plenty of money
Because Guyana is a rich country
The Indian brought with them their culture
They sing and dance while they labor

They British never happy with the Indian lifestyle
The worst of condition was created even for a child.
They Indian believe he that born must die
And that suffering will come to those who lie

By Karran Deokarran

THE UNITED STATE OF AMERICA

They came from every nation to America shore
Because they believe their economic ills can be cure
America is label as the world policeman
Everyone feels safe coming to this great American land

America is a safe place to live with a peace of mind
Opportunity to achieve a lifetime reward of any kind
Every country that says America is very bad
Their people are leaving for America happy and glad

For one to know the world come to America
Talk to people from Asia Europe and Africa
Everyone story is an experience of bad government
In America they are treated humanely with good intent

Thank you, America, for accepting people from every nation
They came to you for salvation because of depression
It did not matter who say you are bad oh great America
None is leaving your shore for Africa or Asia

By Karran Deokarran

HISTORY WILL REMEMBER HIM

He wanted to charter a new course for a great nation He
wanted to reshape America to secure economic salvation
No one understand him he tried several times
He never gives up he is being guided by the divine
He saves this great nation from a third world war
He can understand a real enemy from far
Peace and love always his priority mission
He was born to lead with a great vision
He sees everyone as a friend none his enemy
He is a great fighter guided by his destiny
He always stays awake to watch over evil
He possesses great powers to destroys the devil
On the plaque of history will record his name
Many will have cried who tried to get him defame
He saves a great nation from real poverty
He inherited a nation with a rundown economy
As this great leader embark on his final mission
The wise men start to look at his real position
History will remember him as President Barak Hussein
Obama

By Karran Deokarran 1st Jan 2016

TRIBUTE TO A GREAT MAN

In a land of slavery, a son was born
The year was 1918 for Guyana it was a new dawn
A family rejoice a nation hope have risen
Cheddi Bharat Jagan a name that was chosen
As a little boy he grew with great courage
To send him to the U.S.A. wasn't a disadvantage
His return was like a fire that start to ravage
And Janet by his side ready for his voyage
It wasn't long his mission saw the beginning
And by his side the real fire start sparking
Guyanese joined in their thousands for a great uprising
Everyone knew freedom was coming
The name Cheddi shakes the British crown
Freedom freedom he cried all around
A snake bites him and steals the prize he won
A nation suffers with hatred lust and ruining
A battle for democracy he started
By many intellectual cowards he was assaulted
He breaks the bondage of divide and rule
Peace love and unity was his too

Jagan call to fight the enemy all must join hand
Many of his colleagues run for safer land
History and time have joined his mission
In 1992 the great beyond made a decision
Those who run return to cheer and clap
And to fit themselves in vacant gap
It wasn't long Cheddi real problem began
Which lead him to the great beyond
Many years have pass I miss him a lot
I shared his company many things we chat
Cheddi was a man of great honesty

Many he trusted cast a spell on his dignity
The teaching of Cheddi Jagan became renowned
His call for a new global human order was all around
His vision was to unity Guyanese sons and daughters
History will revere him as a true Mahatma

By Karran P. Deokarran (VICKRAM) March 2011 Florida U.S.A.

HAPPY 95 BIRTHDAY

He born in Africa the richest land on earth
A nation that live in poverty which make him hurt
He set his mind on a sacred mission
He embarks on a peaceful revolution
Tortured and imprisonment for him was nourishment
To destroy evil was his only intent
His admirer gives him hope and courage
As he seeks victory on his sacred voyage

To send brave men to prison is to make them wise
It allowed their consciousness to give other's a surprise
History have never said evil has won any fight
India and Africa are lesson for those of might
His 95th birthday is a lesson for all learned men
Bravery dose not lies in a microphone or a pen
Great men are those who face the battle with love
They stand on their feet and face weapon unresolved
Oh, great Nelson Mandela my salutation to thee
Like Gandhi your mission was to set poverty free
May your courage and love give you strength to live on?
May your act of bravery be man greatest lesson

GOODBYE MANDELA

Like a flower he blossoms in this world
His life and works history will unfold
He departed from his old and weary body
He takes with him the love and admiration of his country
He came into this world like every man
He lives a life of a great human
He lives and work for others
He will be remembered as Africa greatest leader
Great men do not die but leave their body
They live in the heart of Wise men some say it destiny Nelson
Mandela walks the earth with courage and simplicity
Forgiveness, love and reconciliation was his priory
For 27 years he lives in South Africa prison When he
became president, he gives an olive branch a lesson
He believes the world can only be built on love and unity
His mission was freedom and prosperity
Like Mahatma Gandhi and Martin Luther King Nelson
Mandela was a hero a legendary a great human being
He pierces the heart of his enemy with the sword of love
And with Peace and unity apartheid had to remove

Goodbye Nelson Mandela champion of the poor
Your lifestyle will change the minds of evil for sure
The legacy you left millions will cherish
Go rest in peace, god's blessing and best wish

By Karran P. Deokarran

A HUMBLE PRESIDENT

It was 22nd Nov 1963 on the Dallas Street of the U.S.A.
The great America wake up to the call of sympathy
A hero, A state man. A great human had fallen
Only destiny can say why it had to happen.

The bullet that was meant for others
Pierce the heart of the nation most revered Leader As
his body fell to the earth his soul leave with a smile
Great man do not die, killer's think like a child.
50 years later I sit to reflect
On this great American idol with a human intellect He
wanted America to be a great and honorable nation Somebody
feel it was a bad decision. In this evil age good men do not
live long Evil always want to prove right is wrong.
The world is suffering because of many wrong decisions
One such is John. F. Kennedy assassination.
Gandhi leaves his body by assassin bullet.
The Freedom Fighter Martin Luther fell evil did it?
John. F. Kennedy was sent on the same mission.
50 years later his message is America solution

By Karran P. Deokarran

A DREAM

He had a dream a dream for his People
He wanted fair play and justice for all
His heart pain him whenever he sees discrimination,
He then decided to embark on a sacred mission He
preaches of black and white people with red blood
He preaches of unity and loves something everyone should
He wanted a great America for the American People
He believes that with unity nothing is impossible
He embarks on a freedom march to Washington
His enemy have created a plan and took up their position
The assassin's bullet pierces through his loving heart
Another great freedom fighter this body he had to depart
Death can only devour those who have hatred
Martin Luther King JR. was a man of great courage
His departure has brought to the enemy great defeat
His dream has awakened millions on America Street
His death has awakened the world from their long sleep
Freedom Freedom a loud voice cried March on don't weep
Remember me if you wish by loving each other
This will help America and the world to be better

FREEDOM FREEDOM

Freedom Freedom loud and hard they cried
Freedom they wanted from the chain to which they were tied
Freedom they wanted from whip that lashes every day
Freedom from the wound which they receive as pay

They were human why such inhuman treatment
They had their own way of life for which they were sent
No one has the right to slave people for their labor
Nor can there be any forgiveness for such behavior

The African then might have had less intelligence
But the British have proven they had no human sense
They use skill to chain the African for their labor
Today the same African are teachers, Lawyers, and Doctors

The African treatment in Guyana can never be forgotten
The British behavior was inhuman and rotten
The slave master planted hatred into the African brain
Then tell the world African are bad and unclean

I salute the Guyanese African on their freedom anniversary
Let your freedom be a great lesson for every family
Build bridges across the ocean of hatred
Let unity and love brighten your future with good deeds

Reflect on the past and prepare for the future
Remember your courage and strength was your culture
This was taken away from you during slavery
Now is the time to restore it for your bravery

I urge you my Africans Brothers and Sisters
Let not your past destroy your future
Together we must work to make Guyana a land of Paradise
Shun evil politician it's time to unite and become wise

By Karran P. Deokarran

INDIA POWER

There will be another great event in history
This time it will be a British tragedy
Spiritual power sometime remains silent
But reveal itself at the right moment

Very soon there will be trouble in the British crown
Because there is something to India it belongs
The crown will be turning upside down
Until the Koh-I-Noor diamond return to where it belongs

It will not be too late for Britain to ask forgiveness
Rather than to live in distress
India is great for it patient and tolerance
And will accept the koi-in-Noor without vengeance

Our Bible say whatever you sow you shall reap
Our Gita remind us of karma man cannot escape
Our Koran tell us the wicked will not escape Allah power
It is better to do the right thing than too sorry at the last hour

By Karran P. Deokarran

PRICES FOR SUGAR

They beat the Dutch and chase them away
This is how the British went to Guyana and stay
The brought people from Africa in chain
Then put them in the sugar plantation to plant cane

From slavery to indenture labor
Many were subjected to severe beating and torture
This is how the British treat human in Guyana
All the slave master wanted is more sugar

When the African start to rebel
They went to India for people many lies they tell
Come to Guyana life will be better
You will live in bungalow plenty of food and sifting sugar

The Indian were loaded in [boat] the Hesperus and with by
In horrible condition to Guyana they journey
Their arrival in Guyana was a nightmare
They were treated like animal none to see nor hear

Living and working on the estate was horrible
For many livings become unbearable
Many for their children to go to school had join other religion
Other hold on to their culture despite more oppression

The African an Indian unite to fight for freedom
The message was to the British you will have to leave and run
We will take Guyana for our labor
No more British Guyana no more slave master.

Sugar although sweet became bitter in Guyana
Until sugar vanish the nation will continue to suffer
On the sugar plantation lie blood, sweat and tears
Sugar will never profit but yield distrust and fear.

By Karran Deokarran

DEMOCRACIES

Democracy can never be election to elect a Government
Democracy is to manage the affairs with good intent
Democracy can never be a majority vote in parliament
Democracy is consultation and listening to people comment

Democracy is leaders can make decision by the street corner
Democracy is when Government can display good behavior
Democracy is all about truth and honesty
Democracy is the highest discipline in any country

Democracy was never for the rich to tell the poor what is right
Democracy was never for the strong to start any fight
Democracy is to see every nation wealth benefit all equally
Democracy is to allow everyone to live in prosperity

Democracy is fairness and justice which everyone deserved
Democracy is peace fully nation problem can be resolved
Democracy is never for hatred and which hunting
Democracy is allowed participation in development planning

Democracy can never be sanction on any country
Democracy can never be for any nation to go hungry
Democracy is to remove government that become dictator
Democracy is when every nation can unite together

Democracy is for everyone to discuss development
Democracy allowed one to disagreed with good intent
Democracy must display purity love and honesty
Democracy was design by God for man to display sincerity

By Karran P. Deokarran

MY FAITH

544 days in a prison cell
Many stories I live to tell
Beating and tortured were many I beg to die
The supreme lord said son don't cry
I was wrong to think the kidnapper was my enemy
The real culprit I dwell in their company
Many have asked why I am leaving
I know what Guyana will be facing
I live six day and night without food and water
All I wanted to defend the PPP for Guyana future
I lied to the Guyanese nation
And was kick by P.P.P. when they win election
Chedi Jagan was an honest man
The party was highjack by a criminal band
Many have lust for wealth and position
Which lead many good men into a world of corruption
I leave Guyana, so I can free my mind
And to seek guidance from the divine
To Guyana, one day I will return
For the Guyanese people a new day will born

MARRIAGE

The secret of marriage is to understand each other
Prepare to accept worse or better
Trust and confidence will keep marriage together
And in god name marriage will be forever

God created man and woman for each other in the world
Go forth and build a generation they were told
Trust and cherish each other
Everything will be there to full fill your desire

Greed and lust are the enemy of marriage
Oh man you must choose a safe passage
You came for a special purpose oh man
Remember Marriage is god plan

Oh man do not try to gamble with your life
Don't do the wrong thing and blame your wife
The truth will emerge one day
And a huge price you will have to pay

RELIGION AND POLITIC

Politics and religion are a one-way road to success
Practice with honesty it will bring happiness
Politic give guidance for economic achievement
Religion guide man to attain spiritual upliftment
God and man are inseparable
If man live a life that is honorable
Those who sit and wait for tomorrow
Will only achieve great sorrow
Politic guide everyone to attain material development
Health education and social uplift mint
Leaders are appointed with an obligation
To ensure development take place without discrimination
Religion leads man to go back to god
It teaches what will happen if you do bad
Practice religion for peace comfort and happiness
Religion helps everyone to achieve spiritual success
Guyanese a small population crying for land to produce
Government position to rule and abuse
Every government says we will look into your cry
Until it become easier to get a visa and fly

GUYANA INDEPENDENCE

It was 26th May 1966 down came the union jack
In Guyana it will be no more don't ask
Up came the golden arrowhead twirling in the wind
A nation with laughter and joy stood close behind

Wise Leader's look on with a divided mind
The birth of a new nation will be of what kind
The fight for freedom was full of hatred and passion
Wise men asking what it will bring for their nation

The only thing remains from the British oppression
Was the African and Indian culture and tradition
A god given gift for the Guyanese nation
The only path to their final liberation
Fifty years later everyone is asking one question
What have we achieved as a nation?
Hatred, lust, greed, distrust and passion
This we live to treasure as a free nation

Guyana a country with great wealth everywhere
Yet its people living in poverty and fear
Everyone in parliament playing circle tennis game
Fighting for money, power, position and fame

It is sad to say on this Independence Day
The only joy is to live in hope and pray
That one day there will be final liberation
And Guyana will become a free independence nation

By Karran P. Deokarran 26th May 2016.

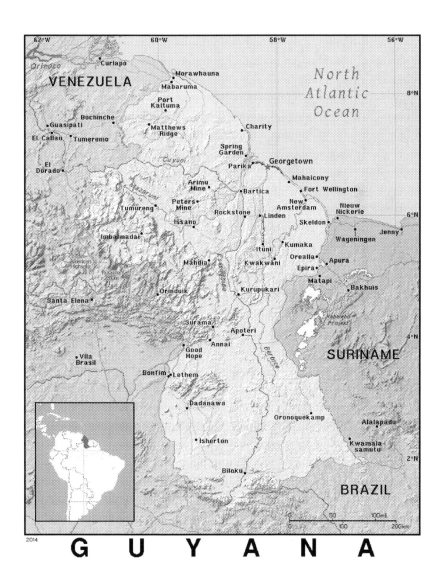

G U Y A N A

TRUTH

Truth is the only weapon to destroy evil
Love the only food for satisfaction
Honesty the only shelter to give comfort Light
Just how light destroy darkness
Truth and Love destroy lies, Hatred and Passion
God is self-discipline

MAN WEAKNESS

Man, greatest weakness is to use his mouth plenty
He forgets he have a brain and how to use it

WISE MAN

The educated man remembers yesterday
The foolish man only cares about today
The wise man looks at yesterday today
And prepare for tomorrow

THE CROWN

The crown was always sacred
It never meant to wear by clown
Clown build missiles to kill man who will die one day

A FAMILY OF HATE & FATE

Man, greatest weakness is failing to try
My story many will ask how and why
A man his wife and kids living happily
Until one day they were about to Part Company

Lust fell into the eyes of the husband
By the time he realizes it was wrong she ties his hand
Then death start too close in and nowhere out
The loving wife stood by his side in tears she shouts

I always cherish and treat him as a loving husband
I pray oh god save him from death hands
Then a god Samaritan came to hear his story
Take him to the house of god and plead for mercy

When mercy was granted joy fill the heart of the wife
The husband begs forgiveness he vow to start a new life
They pledge before god and man to live in unity
And to raise a righteous and loving family

Man must never try to become ungrateful
Especially when they have a wife that is faithful
The lesson can be hard and dangerous
Destruction or death is always a must

Any man who want plenty wife don't marry
It will be a burden you will not able to carry
You will become the laughingstock in history
Your destination will haunt you in the cemetery

By Karran Deokarran

GIVE A WOMEN THE WHITE HOUSE

When Fathers fail their children future
Only mothers can cheer them together When
father's show more concern for strangers
Only a mother can give children a bright future.

Indira Gandhi ruled India; the world greatest democracy
Margret teacher ruled England once the world conquer.
Bandarnike ruled Sri Lanka once the evil Rawan kingdom.
Janet Jagan born American rule Guyana with great courage.

Angela Merkel the German chancellor a brave ruler.
Sheikh Hasina, Bangladesh champion political leader.
Kamla ruled Trinidad the land of the hummingbird.
Portia Simpson, she leads Jamaica forward.

Cristina Fernandez Argentina president a brave woman.
Benazir Bhutto Pakistan leader a great women fighter.
What are we waiting for oh great American civilization?
Only a mother love will save the nation from destruction.

American people a women leader is your future.
An economy would move on under a women leader.
We must show the world; we can lead with confident.
We the world we can have a women president.

Foolish men look for flaws to attack his competitor.
Wise men complement other who join in the race for leader.
Poor minds spend all their time attacking each other
Rich mind always advocate to build a bright future

Hillary Clinton wants to brighter American future.
She is a woman of motherly love she will make a great leader.
Her power and authority lie in her affection for other.
Give her a chance she will bring a bright future

BY Karran P. Deokarran (02/10/2016) U.S.A.

PRAYERS

Prayers help to awaken the conscience
The more silent it is being recite
The greater the effect its carry
Try it every morning

A NATION

A Nation unite together will never suffer
Do not live like parasite on your country
Give your all and live together happy

MAN

When Man loses moral value
Man loses all right to live
In a world full of evil
Such person is considered a walking dead

By Karran P. Deokarran

GUYANESE STOP THE COMEDIAN SHOW

Guyana is a comedian center for politicians Every five years
they elected a Government then pour condemnation
They used their media to condemn their own country They
cried things expensive only rum and beer make them happy
They condemn Burnham and his Government no good
They tell the P.P.P. 2015 no vote you going to hold wood
Now they say Granger Government bad to worst
For how long Guyanese would live with this curse The P.N.C.
spend 28 years in Government trying to be self sufficient
The get rich people selling ban food with excitement The P.P.P.
spend 23 years Familyism and friendships' a new policy
Take taxpayer billions to run the fail sugar economy
God laughing in heaven say let me teach them a lesson
So, he mixes them up in a party to create real confusion
Every day they are crying how things getting bad
Find them in the rum shop dancing happy and gad
Well I took my Rani and went to my beautiful country
Five planes running every day to my lovely Guyana
Guyanese crying the road need two more lanes
They break out the parking meter what new game
So, cry Guyanese cry hard thing in the U.S.A. getting hard
Soon the barrel will stop roll don't get too sad
You are about to face the wall unite to build your destiny
Stop your comedian show help build your country

By Karran Deokarran

DESTINY A GREAT REWARD

Oh, it was a rare dream I ever had
Then the banging on my door later I became sad
And then a scared seen began
Only to know I was in the enemy hand
Guns and soldiers everywhere
First, I thought it was a nightmare
Then a horrible voice I could hear
And suddenly my heart went cold with fear
I was taken out of my bed in the middle of the night
Blind folded I was taken away on a frighten flight
My destination a memory that will be forever
And the memory of the kidnapper torture
While on this scary journey
I ask oh god take care of my family
For I know my mission in this world is over
And this body I will depart through torture
For six days and six nights
Many tortures I with stand by god's might
I survive without food and water
By God Grace I live to tell the world later

Electric shocks and beating everyday
To the enemy nothing I have to say
On my knee I walk on rough stone
My head flush in toilet bowl by men unknown
Each night I would sit and pray
Oh, almighty God come take me away
For in this world no more I wish to stay
The torture and pain increase every day
As I walk from court to prison
On my shoulder I carry the charge of treason
For 544 days I cried in a prison cell

And await the moment a story I have tell
As a Political prisoner the treatment was rough
My wife always says make your mind tough
The prison food was not fit for scavenger
My wife ensures she take care of my hunger
On a wooden floor I lie without cover Sleepless night
Among dangerous prisoner I am being kept
The prison library become my best friend
Trial in the court I await to stand up and defend
If there is anything to praise will be my wife
She was responsible for giving me a second life
In court like sharp steel she pierces the enemy hearts
And tell the judge the enemies have finished their part
Where there is no righteousness in the heart
All beauty in the character depart
Corruption and distrust become a reality in Guyana
None have confidence in any political party
My goal is to see Guyana free and everyone lives in harmony
A united people enjoying peace and prosperity
Then my torture will be my gift to my country
In the name of peace love and unity

By Karran Deokarran USA

FROM LOGI TO BUNGALOW

My fore parent came from India the land of the great
To Guyana they were brought No one know what their faith
On the sugar plantation they had to labor
Living was rough, but where they came from wasn't better
They came with their culture and their tradition
And honesty and truth will remain their religion
The British try to remove from them Hinduism and Islam
They labor in hot sun and rain but maintain their tradition
Some say the Indian were fool with plenty of promises
In Guyana, hard labor greets them with surprise
Other say the Indian do not know to read and write
They were given a contract which was a human plight
What ever happened history will remind us it was destiny
The Indian should be thankful to be on this sacred journey
The Indian who came were seen as indenture labor
But was Islam and Hinduism greatest messenger
Where in the world labor in the field is in air condition Guyana
sugar workers still striking for pay and better position
The British give the African and Indian a country to cherish
Many who left behind in India still live in poverty?
The Indian were given a home which was called Logi
The sing their Koran and Ramayana and live happily
They believe from the sweat of thy brow thou shall eat bread
Their hard work is to remind their offspring not to beg
After five years the Indian were given a chance to return
They remain on the sugar plantation become a norm
They work hard and save their money for their future happiness
Drinking their daro and smoking their chillum take their stress
My salutation to my fore parent who to come to Guyana
To the British I say thank you for bringing them out of
India

Today there offspring have spread across the
world with their religion and culture
They are now some of the world best lawyer, doctor
and political leader Every writers and historian are
looking for the torture that was done on the Indian
No one never examine to see what the
Indian have brought with them
Torture is happening all over the world every
day who has the courage to say
The Indian come to Guyana be remembered as a historical day
They were given Logi to live; they ask God for his guidance
God give them faith and courage for their existence
Today their offspring are living in comfort and happiness with
bungalow, car and plenty of money without any stress
Many writers are still searching for the (kala pani) black water
And what happen in the with by and Hesperus while the
Indian was travelers
Today the Indian running to the White man country
They leave freedom, living in basement and
working in condition of modern slavery
Man have proven today that real slavery endowed in
Bachelor, master's and Degree
The wise man walks with his conscience
and slave for people and country
The Logi people had no certificate they had truth, love and honesty
Their hard work become bungalow and will remain for eternity

IT WILL HAPPEN

Destruction is raising its ugly head
Honesty and love are dead
Corruption will cause the third world war
Deadly missile will fire from near and far
Two powers will be fighting for supremacy
A war will start unknowing
One side will be fighting to protect religion
The other wants to protect its economic position
Millions of people will die
Million loud will be their cry
The earth will be filled with human blood
For righteousness it will be good
This war will be between the east and the west
Everyone will put their weapon to the test
Some will fight in the name of god
Others saying, they want to rid the world of bad
In this war there will be no winner
A new generation will breed fresh air
They will live happy without any fear

By Karran P. Deokarran

A CARING HOSPITAL

A visit to the New York Methodist hospital
My Doctor Bhambhani second call
First visit I had two steins in two arteries
The second time to review the artery ability
The Doctor preform their duty with great care
The nurses love and affections can be seen everywhere
The staff attend patient with a smile
Management show great care with a human style
The environment brings to one real happiness
Entering the hospital remove on distress
By the time the doctor determines one sickness
There is a feeling of comfort and happiness
The New York Methodist Hospital a caring institution
Handle your medical problem and offer solution
Jesus once said gives help and care to others
The Almighty will provide your care forever
My praises to all of you great workers
Continue to give service with a smile to others
Doctors Nurse and staff always be loving and caring
Your blessing from God will be everlasting

By Karran P. Deokarran March 2013 U.S.A.

THIS I SHOULD DO

For a purpose I was given this human body
I should use it with dignity
My duty to take care of all limbs and properties
And to enjoyed living in human liberties

I choose to live like a mango tree
To give to others what was given for free
A mango tree gives it fruit freely and receive more
This is how I prepared to live this life for sure

A mango tree never tells anyone how much it gives
Sometimes it loses it limbs but still give to live
If a human can live like a mango tree
Gives to others with a loving heart free

Like a mango tree my existence I will try to design
Give to others no question of any kind
To the mango tree I bow in salutation
Live like a mango tree and have salvation

By Karran Deokarran 03/11/2017 U.S.A.

HONESTY THE PATH TO SUCCESS

Every evening on a busy liberty street corner
There I share the company of Guyanese Brothers
The gathering always engages in diverse discussions
The enemy of progress will ask agitating question

It's a joy to see how political spies take their position
Playing with cell phone taping discussion
Their support against evil always encouraging
All their interest is what everyone saying

Guyanese have a history of betraying others for nothing
With sweet words and smile the do the misleading
In Guyana and north America is the same behavior
Many in religious garbs robing others

When political spies start to spy on each other
Over a cup of chai tea, I will watch with laughter
In America Guyanese searching for a new President
They are runaway coward with no honest intent

By Karran Deokarran

70

A MESSAGE

Some crazy people say it Hurricane Sandy
Others say she is powerful and windy
Some say its Mother nature at work
Some is asking why only some get hurt

Whatever everyone has to say
It's a lesson for the world to learn in one day
Man must never boost about power
The Almighty God can Strike at any hour

There are nuclear missiles every where
A small hurricane came every on running in fear
A short message God send
Oh Man do good and stop pretend

We must never try hurting each other
We can learn from all the sacred scripture
Stop boost about who is powerful
Those who remain alive should be thankful

By Karran Deokarran

OBAMA CARES

He became United State 44th President it wasn't a coincident
He was elected by the people no fraud no incident
He inherits the white house which was in a mess
He set out to find answers to remove the nation distress
He preaches love no hatred for the nation
He wanted answer for the poor and middle-class salvation
He had to save an economy already in bankruptcy
He had to bail out the business to save the economy
He brought health care to twenty million American
He created job and education for the nation
He saves the housing sector from Bankruptcy
He instills hopes and confidence in the nation economy
He believed the nation leader must be a good father
He wanted a safe enviourment to unite the world together
He hates racial discrimination and corruption He had to
fight elected leaders who want to stop his mission
Farewell to you Mr. President Barak Obama a great leader
You give every American hope for a bright future
You try to stop wars you are a man of great care
Your legacy is the American dream wise men will share

By Karran Deokarran

REAL POLITICIAN

Those who want Political office give up family and friends
Their motives must be country and people to defend
A good politician first gives up wealth and pleasure
His mind set should be governance for a bright future

A politician without truth and honesty is poison for a nation
Ready to rule with faith in thy self-full of corruption
A Politician is born with a golden brain not a golden spoon
Will not go after enemy but reach for the moon

Real politician belongs to a world where few men are born
A world full of joy without any hatred or thorns
A real politician ruled with a steadfast mind
A false politician sees the nation as blind

A real politician never looks for comfort any where
His people welfare and happiness he cares
If the world is to be a place which is good and pure
The choice of a good political leader is the only cure

By Karran Deokarran

A JOURNEY BACK HOME

Thirty first of March two thousand and eighteen
To beautiful Guyana a land where my birth was given
To celebrate my 60th Birthday with the divine
Paying tribute to Mother Earth for my up brining
Religious ceremony had always my mission
Paying respect to God preforming puja my only intention
Among friends and relatives, the ceremony began
It was a day of contentment and satisfaction
Then a tour across the country would reveal many thing
Improvement in the social sector a new beginning
There are still the language thing bad waiting for the barrel
And the opposition every day in a quarrel
Business going up everywhere with everything for sale
Because of large scale migration purchasing another tale
Everywhere I go the tune is thing really bad
Three cars in the garage all the night spot busy non sad
This the story of my lovely Guyana past and present
Now listen as I unfold the future and what I intend
Guyana will return to its glory with honesty and justice
All the bad politician will be exiled, and honesty will practice

MY GUYANA

The hidden story of my Guyana a great nation
The Dutch Man lay the foundation
The British came, seized and Rule
The African and Indian make them a fool
The Dutch Man hard working and progressive
Cotton their main produce very expensive
Gold coin was their money
They never lust for others country
The British invade beat and chase them away
Then brought African to slave without pay
The British create the sugar industry
To produce wealth for England to be happy
When the African start to rebel against management
The British brought Indians to work with slave treatment
Unity in the workplace create a new tradition
That will shake the mighty British Position
The African and Indian brought their culture and tradition
It's a secret weapon in the scheme of migration
It's can force any one to change their position
The British try every trick to maintain their domination
Destiny came in to play, the fight for freedom began
Two leaders were created Burnham and Jagan
The British finally agreed to give Guyana Freedom
A new trick Independence and race division
Frustration was created among the two leaders
Fighting among the major race will be forever
Religion and culture lost its position
Our fore parents were not remembering at the inauguration
Guyana secured independence and frustration
Our Moto one People one Nation one Destiny bear corruption
The spirit of our fore parents is still roaming everywhere
No Government can rule with stability and care

By Karran P. Deokarran (Vickram)
23rd February 2018 U.S.A.

MARIJUANA

Marijuana like every other plant was created by God
Because he wanted his children to be happy and glad
In its leaves hidden all the medicinal qualities
It's a food that will keep you strong and healthy

For those who don't wish to live long and strong
Smoke marijuana it damages the brain memory gone
Marijuana become the devil tools when smoking
Marijuana become the Angel tools when drinking

Marijuana was declared illegal by the illegal society
Who prepare the sick world for their property
Manufacturing tablets and called it illness cure
Making millions while you going to the cemetery for sure

If humanity is to free from all illness and pain
Drink marijuana tea keep you healthy and a strong brain
Live a long and healthy life drinking marijuana
It was created by God for you and your family

By karran Deokarran 5/6/18

HIS VISION FOR A NATION

He was task with leading a newborn nation
He was given a task to maintain the master division
His opponent couldn't understand and behave as opposition
Which give the master a chance to protect their division

This young leader silently wants to unite the nation
The cold war was ruling with betrayal and assassination
His plan was development through self-sacrifice
The opposition keep protesting the division find success

To keep the division the master used many cunning tricks
Government official were encouraged into corrupt politic
This leader had great hopes to build a great nation
Only wake up to learn he must fight for his own salvation

A wise opposition would have used his followers to forge relation
Work to unite the people against the master intention This
would have strengthen the leader position for this nation
Two great race great race lost their happiness and tradition

This great leader understands the master intention
No ruler would easily give up a country to please it nation
Had the opposition understand the master true intention
He would have eradicated lust and ego and forge unification
No power can remove or destroyed destiny
Two men were born to lead a nation that suffer greatly
Both did their job and died mysteriously This nation
must learn from the past if the future is to be happy
This great country was owned by the British and is called
Guyana
The two major races came from Africa and India
At independence the British choose L.F.S. Burnham to rule Chedi
B. Jagan become the opposition the British made them fool

History will remember Burnham a man with great vision
Chedi B. Jagan the greatest leader to be an opposition
Burnham wanted to make Guyana a great nation
The British give Independence and create division Our fore
parent fight for liberation and shake the British crown
The British used Burnham and Jagan and make everyone a clown
Our fore parent spirit still wondering and creating confusion
Freedom they seek before Guyana get salvation

Karran, Nalenine, Latchmi, Menakshi, Bhanmatie, Chuniram.

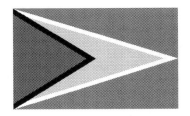

Guyana where my mission begins
From the United State my message was able to spread
Guyana will always be in my heart
The U.S.A. allow me to touch the world with
words of love Karran P. Deokarran

Contact Information
Name Karran Persaud Deokarran (Vickram)
Email deokarrank@yahoo.com
Gmail deokarrak@gmail.com
Face Book Karran Deokarran
Mailing address U.S.A. 471 Autumn Ave Brooklyn N.Y. U.S.A.
Ph 631-829-2623, 347-737-4673
Guyana Lot 6 Bath Mahaicony Reg. 5 E.C.D. Guyana
Ph. 592 258 0117

Printed in the United States
By Bookmasters